JOHN MERRILL'S STAFFORDSHIRE

MOORLAND CH/

by

JOHN N. MERRILL

Maps and photographs

by John N. Merrill

a J.N.M.PUBLICATION

1988

i

a J.N.M. PUBLICATION

JNM PUBLICATIONS,
WINSTER,
MATLOCK,
DERBYSHIRE.
DE4 2DQ

Conceived, edited, typeset, designed, marketed and distributed by John N. Merrill.

© Text and Route — John N. Merrill 1988

© Maps and photographs — John N. Merrill 1988

First Published — May 1988

ISBN 0 907496 67 9

Meticulous research has been undertaken to ensure that this publication is highly accurate at the time of going to press. The publishers, however, cannot be held responsible for alterations, errors or omissions, but they would welcome notification of such for future editions.

Printed by: Commercial Colour Press, London E7 0EW

Set in Futura — medium and bold.

ABOUT JOHN N. MERRILL

John combines the characteristics and strength of a mountain climber with the stamina and athletic capabilities of a marathon runner. In this respect he is unique and has to his credit a whole string of remarkable long walks. He is without question the world's leading marathon walker.

Over the last ten years he has walked more than 60,000 miles and successfully completed ten walks of at least 1,000 miles or more.

His six major walks in Great Britain are -
Hebridean Journey .... 1,003 miles
Northern Isles Journey .... 913 miles
Irish Island Journey .... 1,578 miles
Parkland Journey .... 2,043 miles
Lands End to John o'Groats .... 1,608 miles
and in 1978 he became the first person (permanent Guinness Book of Records entry) to walk the entire coastline of Britain — 6,824 miles in ten months.

In Europe he has walked across Austria — 712 miles — hiked the Tour of Mont Blanc, completed High Level Routes in the Dolomites, and the GR20 route across Corsica in training! In 1982 he walked across Europe — 2,806 miles in 107 days — crossing seven countries, the Swiss and French Alps and the complete Pyrennean chain — the hardest and longest mountain walk in Europe, with more than 600,000 feet of ascent!

In America he used the the world's longest footpath — The Appalachian Trail -2,200 miles — as a training walk. He has walked from Mexico to Canada via the Pacific Crest Trail in record time — 118 days for 2,700 miles.

During the summer of 1984, John set off from Virginia Beach on the Atlantic coast, and walked 4,226 miles without a rest day, across the width of America to Santa Cruz and San Francisco on the Pacific Ocean. His walk is unquestionably his greatest achievement, being, in modern history, the longest, hardest crossing of the USA in the shortest time — under six months (178 days). The direct distance is 2,800 miles.

Between major walks John is out training in his own area — the Peak District National Park. As well as walking in other parts of Britain and Europe he has been trekking in the Himalayas five times. He has created more than ten challenge walks which have been used to raise more than £250,000 for charity. From his own walks he raised over £80,000. He is author of more than ninety books, most of which he publishes himself. His book sales are in excess of 2 million.

CONTENTS

ELLASTONE

INTRODUCTION

I have been aware of the scenic beauty of the Staffordshire Moorlands and especially the stunning Churnet Valley. I had long wanted to write a book on the walks in the area and this ambition was fulfilled in 1987 with my Short Walk book. This was later followed that year by my Canal Walks Vol Two book which included the delightful Caldon Canal. I am working on a Long Circular Walk book, but in the meantime I wanted to extend my Challenge Walk series and so have added this one!

As with all my challenge walks, I endeavour to make them strenuous, but linking together my favourite parts of the region. After several forays into the area I finally decided upon my route and set off from Oakamoor in late October 1987. Eight hours later in perfect weather I had walked the route and was rather stunned at the high quality of the scenery. I shall not forget the long autumn shadows of the Churnet Valley from Toothill Rock. With the walk completed I was still slightly unhappy about two of the areas and after a few more forays found the best routes.

I thoroughly enjoyed the walk and its tremendous variety of views, woodland, river, village and canal locations. I can only hope that you experience an equally perfect day for your walk and see for yourself the magnificent scenery of the Churnet Valley. The view from the Weaver Hills on a clear day is among the top ten in England! Have a good walk and let me know how you got on!

HAPPY WALKING!

John N. Merrill.

JOHN N. MERRILL
Winster, Derbyshire 1988.

1

CHURNET VALLEY CAR PARK — OAKAMOOR

ABOUT THE WALK -

Starting from Oakamoor you ascend Stoney Dale to reach the woodland of Hawksmoor Nature Reserve. You descend to East Wall Farm following a segment of the Staffordshire Way to the River Churnet and Kingsley Holt. Here you descend to the river and ascend to Leys before passing between houses and descending to Froghall Wharf. Leaving the valley behind you gradually ascend to Hoften's Cross and the Weaver Hills. After following the hill's crest you descend to Stanton and gain the lesser known but attractive Ordley Dale. Passing through Ellastone you regain the Churnet Valley and pass Crumpwood Weir before walking beneath Alton Castle — Staffordshire's Rhineland. You ascend to Alton and Toot Hill Rock whose view is impressive. Now in woodland you gain the aptly named Rambler's Retreat Cafe and walk up Ousal Dale. At its head you descend for the final time to Oakamoor and car park.

ENTRANCE PLAQUE TO HAWKSMOOR NATURE RESERVE

2

HOW TO DO IT -

The whole route is covered by the Ordnance Survey Map — 1:25,000 Pathfinder Series Sheet No SK 04/14 — Ashbourne and the Churnet Valley.

The walk is devised to be done in a single day, allowing between 8 — 12 hours. It is not a race but a walk to be enjoyed at your own pace and can be done over a weekend or two outings. For those who complete the entire walk a special four-colour embroidered badge and signed certificate by John Merrill is available from JNM Publications. A master record of all who walk the route is also maintained by them. A further register is kept at the Staffordshire Peak Arts Centre, whose door you pass nearly at the halfway point.

The whole route has been carefully mapped, and you should have no difficulty in walking round. You should always carry the 1:25,000 O.S. map for further clarification if unsure of your way, or in bad weather on the Weaver Hills where a compass would be useful to confirm your true direction. The whole route follows rights of way and does include a small amount of road walking. This is unavoidable because of the lack or poor quality of one or two rights of way. But this in no way spoils the enjoyment of the walk.

There are several inns along the way on or close to the route, as can be seen in the Amenities section, together with accommodation and campsites. The route crosses several roads where backup parties could be waiting with moral support and food and drink. Alton has all the facilities you need and is basically the only place on the walk for everything except Oakamoor, where you begin and end.

STAFFORDSHIRE PEAK ARTS CENTRE

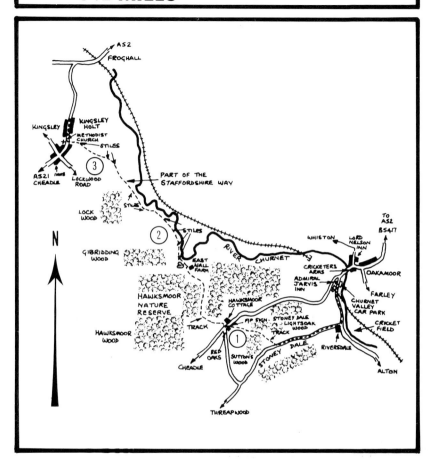

OAKAMOOR — Opposite the car park, the grassy picnic area is the site of Thomas Bolton's copper works. Oakamoor had been a major industrial area for several centuries. In 1790 Thomas Patten and Co. had a large copper-rolling mill. Later this was purchased by Bolton's who in 1856 produced the first Atlantic cable here. The firm expanded considerably but a century later in 1963 it was closed down and buisness was concentrated at the huge Froghall works.

HAWKSMOOR NATURE RESERVE — 250 acres and officially opened in 1933. More than 40 species of birds have been sighted here.

OAKAMOOR TO KINGSLEY HOLT — 3½ MILES
- allow 1½ hours

ABOUT THE SECTION — First you ascend a narrow lane up Stoney Dale before walking through Sutton's Wood and onto Hawksmoor Wood. Here you join the Staffordshire Way, which you follow past the delightfully situated East Wall Farm and across fields near the River Churnet to Kingsley Holt. ¼ mile off the route in the village are two inns. The whole section is a perfect curtain raiser to the countryside to be walked through on this walk.

WALKING INSTRUCTIONS — Turn left out of the car park and in ⅓ mile at the first road junction, in front of the house "Riversdale", turn right along the lane up Stoney Dale, passing Stoneydale Farm on your right. Keep on this lane for ½ mile to a path sign — "Hawksmoor ½ mile." Here turn right and continue ascending through the trees on a track. At the top bear left on the track to the road at Hawksmoor. Pass "Red Oaks" on your left and cross the road to the pillared entrance into Hawksmoor Nature Reserve. Follow the track and descend through woodland and in ½ mile approach East Wall Farm. As indicated by path signs, keep to the left of the farm before nearing the farm pond.

You are now on a section of the Staffordshire Way, and from the pond gain a stile in the righthand corner of the field. The path is faint but for the next ¾ mile you keep near the River Churnet on your right, but keeping a more direct line than its weaving course. The route is well stiled and in ½ mile cross a footbridge over a brook. After the next stile you move away from the river and begin gently ascending, guided by Staffordshire Way signs. Cross three footbridges in the next ¼ mile. Shortly after the last one reach a stile where you bear left on a defined path to the road — A521 — at Kingsley Holt, opposite the Methodist church. A little to your left round the corner are two inns!

EAST WALL FARM POND

KINGSLEY HOLT TO FROGHALL WHARF — 2 MILES

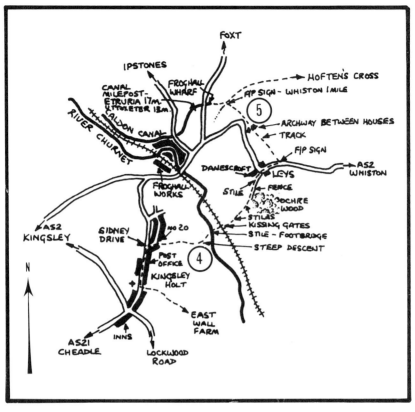

FOXT

IPSTONES

HOFTEN'S CROSS

CANAL MILEPOST-
ETRURIA 17m.
UTTOXETER 13m.

FROGHALL WHARF

F/P SIGN - WHISTON 1 MILE

(5)

RIVER CHURNET

CALDON CANAL

ARCHWAY BETWEEN HOUSES

TRACK

F/P SIGN

DANESCROFT

LEYS

A52 WHISTON

FROGHALL WORKS

STILE

FENCE

OCHRE WOOD

STILES

KISSING GATES

A52 KINGSLEY

SIDNEY DRIVE

No 20

STILE - FOOTBRIDGE

STEEP DESCENT

N

POST OFFICE

(4)

KINGSLEY HOLT

EAST WALL FARM

A521 CHEADLE

INNS

LOCKWOOD ROAD

CALDON CANAL MILEPOST AT FROGHALL WHARF

6

KINGSLEY HOLT TO FROGHALL WHARF — 2 MILES
- allow 50 minutes

ABOUT THE SECTION — Good path all the way as you descend to the River Churnet and ascend to Leys. Here you walk along a track and between the houses to just above Froghall Wharf. If time permits it is well worth descending to your left to the Caldon Canal to see its tranquil setting.

WALKING INSTRUCTIONS — At the road in Kingsley Holt turn right down it for ¼ mile. Just past the Post Office on your right turn right into Sidney Drive. Beside house No 20 turn right onto the signed footpath — Whiston Bridge. Pass through three stiles, and close to Banktop you descend on a defined path to the footbridge — Whiston Bridge. Pass through a kissing gate and ascend the track in Ochre Wood to a stile. On the other side in open fields keep the fence on your right and in ¼ mile reach the A52 road in Leys, close to Danescroft house. Keep ahead up the A52 for a few yards to the first track on your left; a signposted footpath. After just over ¼ mile reach a row of houses with "Beware of Dogs" sign. Keep straight ahead through the archway between the houses and descend to a sharp bend in the A52 road. Keep to the right of it to a stile and follow the line of an old railway down to a track junction close to Froghall Wharf. Diagonally left is the path down to Froghall Wharf.

CALDON CANAL — Primarily a branch of the Trent & Mersey Canal built in 1779 and is 17 miles long from Froghall to Etruria. Primarily used to carry limestone from Froghall. The section from Froghall to Uttoxeter was built in 1811 but has now all but disappeared. A particularly fine remnant will be seen near Crumpwood Weir.

ARCHWAY BETWEEN HOUSES, NEAR LEYS

FROGHALL WHARF TO HOFTEN'S CROSS — 3½ MILES

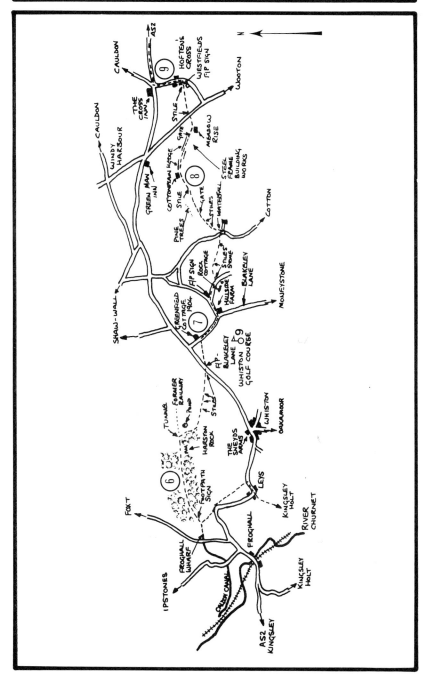

FROGHALL WHARF TO HOFTEN'S CROSS — 3½ MILES
Allow 1½ hours

ABOUT THE SECTION — You ascend out of the valleys to high ground full of surprising views as you near the Weaver Hills. Hoften's Cross is an important staging point, and although not quite half way, it does contain an inn and a restaurant!

WALKING INSTRUCTIONS — At the track junction turn right along the track for a few yards before turning right, at the footpath sign, and ascending the line of a dismantled railway line. Ascend this for ½ mile past Harston Rocks to a footpath crossroads just after. Here turn right on a path, noticing a tunnel under the railway on your left. The path is often overgrown in summer as you curve round high above a stream on woodland. Keep the stream below you on your left and in ¼ mile reach a stile and open fields. Keep the field boundary on your left to reach all the stiles and pass several large water troughs. In just over ¼ mile gain the A52 road.

Cross to your left to the path sign — "Blakeley Lane." The path line is faint as you walk on the immediate right of a brick chequerboard house. The other side is gritstone blocks. Just after the path is hedge and fenced, with Whiston Golf Course on your right. At Blakeley Lane with Greenfield Cottage dated 1904 on your left, turn right along the lane and in ¼ mile left past Hillside Farm on a lane. In 150 yards bear right at the footpath sign, with a prominent rock outcrop on your right, and pass Rock Cottage. Just afterwards on your left is a stone stile. Go through this and descend the field to another stone stile. Over this bear right to another stile and keep the wall on your right and cross a further field towards some houses. Turn left in front of them to a gate and lane.

Turn right along the lane for a few yards and turn left onto the farm drive and left immediately through the stile and ascend the field to a stile. On your right is a small waterfall fed by a pond behind. Keep to the righthand edge of the next field to a gated stile with house just ahead. The pathline is faint but keep the field boundary on your left and head for the top corner of the field and gate. Through this keep the field edge on your left and head towards a mound with pine trees at the back. Keep to the righthandside of the mound to a stile. Continue ahead ascending and walk up a hedged incline to the house, Cottonplain. Don't go through the stile but turn right keeping the hedge on your left, then on your right and then left again. As you near the house ahead (Meadow Rise) after three fields ascend a metal gate and reach the farm/works road. On your right is a steel frame building works. Turl left past Meadow Rise and gain a minor road. Go straight across to a white painted wooden stile and continue along the lefthand side of the field to a stile and enter Westfields in Hoften's Cross. Turn left along the road to the A52 road and the Cross Inn.

HOFTEN'S CROSS TO STANTON — 4½ MILES

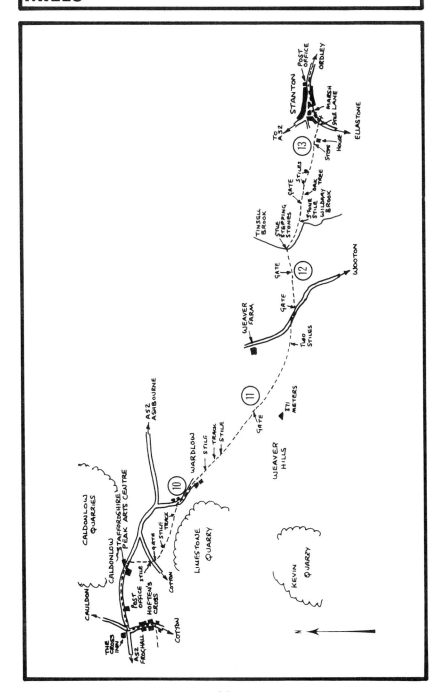

HOFTEN'S CROSS TO STANTON — 4½ MILES
- allow 1¾ hours.

ABOUT THE SECTION — ½ a mile of road walking along the A52 which, although regrettable to have to do, does bring you to the Staffordshire Peak Arts Centre where a Challenge Register is kept and there is Lindy's Kitchen to fortify you. But, the main reason for road walking is simply because there is no other way, as quarries on either side of the road have "gobbled up " the rights of way. Sad though it is, you are about to attain one of the finest view points in Britain, the Weaver Hills. The views on clear days are incredible with Wales on the skyline. You can also have a "count the power stations competition"! I have counted at least twelve. You descend from the hill through fields to the unspoilt village of Stanton.

WALKING INSTRUCTIONS — Turn right along the A52 past the Post Office and Arts Centre — a former school and where the pavement ends. Continue along the A52 for a further 80 yards to the start of the second field past the farm on your right. There is no stile here but there is a gap in the fence where you ascend the small wall. Go diagonally across the field to your left and ⅔rds of the way across the field boundary is on your right. A little further reach a stile and minor road. Go through the gate opposite and keep the field edge on your left. At the bottom ascend a stile and turn left onto a track with the quarry on your right. At the end of the track turn right onto the quarry road Keep on the road round to your left, past the ruined houses of Wardlow, and soon attain a fenced track. Keep on this with views of the summits of the Weaver Hills ahead. Keep the field edge on your left and gain all the stiles. In 1¼ miles from the quarry road reach a lane from Wooton and turn right along it. A few yards later at the cattle grid turn left through the gate and descend the field to a gate. Continue descending to Tinsell Brook with stile and stepping stones. Turn right with the brook on your right to the next stile. You are now heading almost due east to the village of Stanton ¾ mile away. First the wall on your left then right after the next stile to reach another stile. Cross the farm track to a gate and continue ahead past an oak tree on your right to stiles. You gradually begin to descend towards a solitary house with a stile and steps on the left of it. Descend into a hollow and continue ahead to Field Lane gained by a stile opposite the church. Turn left into Stanton and right almost immediately along Marsh Lane.

THE CROSS INN

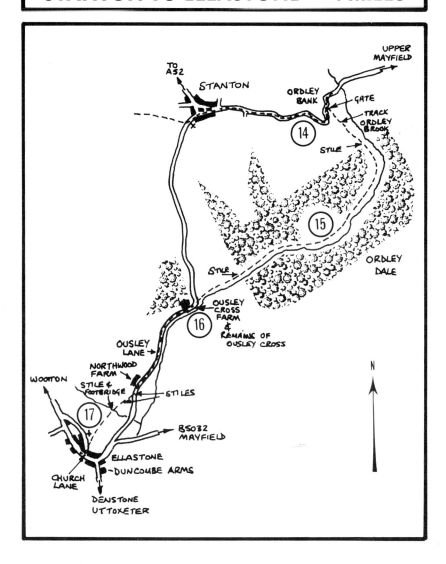

STANTON TO ELLASTONE — 4 MILES
- allow 1½ hours.

ABOUT THE SECTION — You return to woodland and dales as you descend to the Ordley Brook and walk through Stanton Wood to Ousley. A short road walk is followed by a walk across the fields to Upper Ellastone.

WALKING INSTRUCTIONS — Continue through Stanton on Marsh Lane past the Post Office and in ½ mile begin descending the road down Ordley Bank. After rounding a sharp lefthand corner descend steeply and after about 50 yards leave the road at the gate and track on your right. Follow this defined grass track keeping left after ¼ mile and soon gain a stile at the edge of woodland. The path is defined for the next 1½ miles to Ousley but, unlike the dales near Alton, is not walked so often and in summer can be a little overgrown. After 1¼ miles reach a stile and open field with the woodland on your right. Continue on the path to the road — Ousley Lane, near Ousley Cross Farm. Gain the road beside the footpath sign — Mayfield. Turn left along Ousley Lane for ½ mile to Northwood Farm. On your right is Ousley Cross Farm and you can see the cross base and shaft just inside the garden. The cross is believed to have been a boundary marker for Calwich Abbey near Ellastone. Immediately past the buildings of Northwood Farm turn right up the incline to a stile. Cross the field keeping straight ahead to a stile. After this soon reach another and a footbridge. Ahead can be seen the church and simply heading towards it will bring the stiles on your way. At the churchyard wall go through the kissing gate and walk around the lefthand side of the church to the lane. Turn left to the road. A little to your left is the Duncombe Arms.

WEAVER HILLS FROM NEAR ELLASTONE

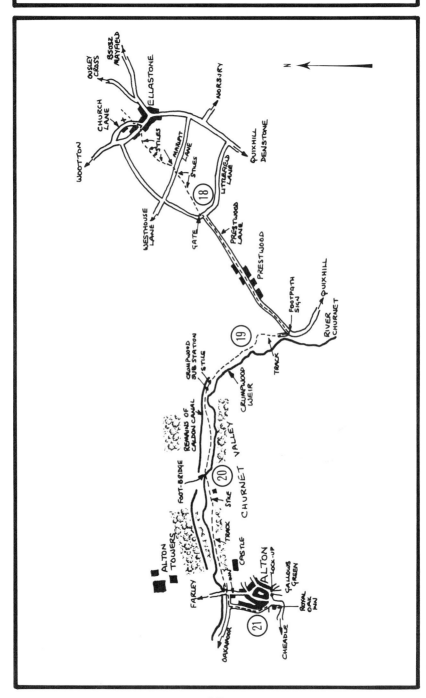

ELLASTONE TO ALTON — 4 MILES
- allow 1½ hours

ABOUT THE SECTION — Ahead can be seen the wooded Churnet Valley crowned on either side by imposing buildings. First you cross the fields to Prestwood Lane, which you then walk along to Prestwood. Shortly afterwards you walk along the road to Crumpwood Weir, picking up the line of the Caldon Canal. You cross the River Churnet and walk beneath Alton Castle to Alton, ready for the final stunning part of the route! There are inns here to give you your final encouragement!

WALKING INSTRUCTIONS — Gaining the main road in Ellastone, just down from the church, turn right and 20 yards later turn left onto a drive and in 20 yards where it meets a gate on your left is a stile by the hedge. Go over this and cross the field to the righthand corner to another stile. Bear right slightly to gain the next stile and after this keep the field boundary on your right to the next stile. Continue ascending to the next stile and Marlpit Lane. Cross to your right to a stile and cross the field to your right to a stile just round a corner in the field. Descend the next field leftwards to a stile and just after reach a gate and gain a road T junction. Keep ahead on Prestwood Lane and follow it past the houses in ½ mile of the village of Prestwood. There are three rights of way on your right as you walk along, but as you can see the hedge has grown over the stone stiles! I have tried following them, once ending up at Alligator Farm, where a notice told me — "Tresspassers will be eaten!" For a moment I thought I was in Florida!

Continue along the lane and about ¼ mile past the last house where the road turns sharp left turn right at the footpath sign onto a track. Follow this, across a tarmaced road and walk along the Waterboard track/road to Crumpwood Weir ½ mile away. Continue past the weir on your left and soon notice the remnants of the Caldon Canal on your right and a splendid canal bridge. Just after is the Crumpwood Switching Station. Keep to the right of it to a stile and kissing gate beyond. You now enter a large field with the River Churnet on your left. Keep in the middle of the field for ⅓ mile to a footbridge over the river. Cross this and bear right and ascend gradually to a stile and farm track. Bear right along this beneath the castle to the road in Alton. Keep ahead past The Talbot Inn and in 50 yards turn left and ascend the lane to West View just before the Royal Oak Inn and turn right onto the path leading down to a walled track. The track can also be reached via the inn.

ALTON — The castle dates back to Saxon times. The principal builder was Bertram de Verdun in the 12th century, but little remains today. The present building, now a preparatory school, was built in the 1840's and designed by Pugin. He was very active on the other side of the valley building Alton Towers for the Shrewsburys. Following a visit to Germany, the Earl of Shrewsbury decided that the ruined castle should be rebuilt like a German Rhineland one; the result today is very similar. Near the centre of the village is the Round House, the village lock-up built in 1830. Alton Towers is the work of the Earls of Shrewsbury. The gardens are considered to be the finest in the country and are the work of Capability Brown. Today they are part of Europe's finest leisure park; Britain's answer to Disneyland!

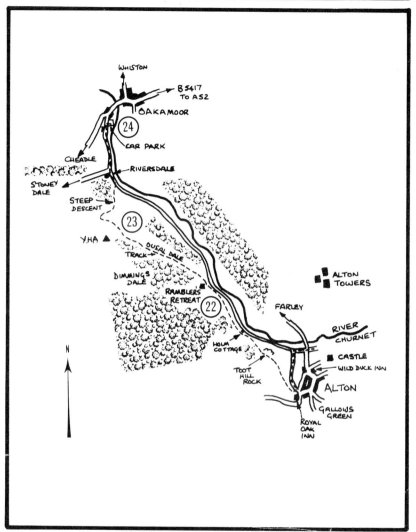

WHISTON

B 5417
TO A52

OAKAMOOR

(24)

CAR PARK

CHEADLE

RIVERSDALE

STONEY DALE

STEEP DESCENT

(23)

Y.H.A. ▲

OUSAL DALE

TRACK

DIMMINGS DALE

RAMBLERS RETREAT

(22)

FARLEY

RIVER CHURNET

HOLM COTTAGE

ALTON TOWERS

■ CASTLE

WILD DUCK INN

TOOT HILL ROCK

ALTON

GALLOWS GREEN

ROYAL OAK INN

N

DIMMINGSDALE YOUTH HOSTEL

16

ALTON TO OAKAMOOR — 3 MILES
- allow 1¼ hours

ABOUT THE SECTION — The last lap, and a stunning walk with superlative views of the Churney Valley, before walking through the wooded Ousal Dale. You can call in at the Rambler's Retreat on the way! You descend steeply through the trees to reach the road at the entrance of Stoney Dale, where you began a few hours ago!

WALKING INSTRUCTIONS — Walk along the walled lane for little over ¼ mile to a sharp lefthand bend with a stile on your right. Go through this and gain Toothill Rock and its remarkable view. Turn left along the woodland edge on the path past the rocks and descend to the road passing the footpath sign — Alton ½ mile. Walk along the road for a few yards before turning slightly left onto the track past Holm Cottage — footpath signed, Dimmingsdale ¾ mile. Keep on the track for ¼ mile but where it bears left keep right and descend the path to the Rambler's Retreat cafe. Turn left but not sharp left and walk up the track to your right along Ousal Dale, passing the mill ponds on your left. Keep on the track gently ascending through the pine trees. ½ mile from the mill ponds reach a footpath crossroads; to your left is Dimmingsdale Youth Hostel and Staffordshire Way signs. Turn right and gain a walled track which bears right towards a solitary house. Before you get there turn left through the stile and keep the wall on your right for a few yards before turning left and descending the steep but well defined path through woodland to the Red Road from Alton, by a water tank. Turn left passing the entrance to Stoney Dale and Riversdale and continue ahead on the road retracing your steps back to the car park — journey's end alas!

EVENING VIEW FROM TOOT HILL ROCK

LOG

DATE .... TIME STARTED .... TIME COMPLETED ....

ROUTE POINT	MILE No	TIME		COMMENTS WEATHER
		Arr.	Dep.	
OAKAMOOR	0			
HAWKSMOOR	1			
RIVER CHURNET	2			
KINGSLEY HOLT	3½			
RIVER CHURNET	4			
LEYS	4½			
FROGHALL WHARF	5½			
HARSTON ROCK	6½			
GREENFIELD COTTAGE	7			
COTTONPLAIN	8			
HOFTEN'S CROSS	9			
STAFFS. PEAK ARTS CENTRE	9½			
WARDLOW	10			
WEAVER HILLS	11			
TINSELL BROOK	12¼			
STANTON	13½			
ORDLEY BANK	14			
ORDLEY DALE	15			
OUSLEY CROSS	16			
ELLASTONE	17			
LITTLEFIELD LANE	18			

PRESTWOOD	18½				
CRUMPWOOD WEIR	19½				
RIVER CHURNET FOOT-BRIDGE	20				
ALTON	21				
TOOT HILL ROCK	21½				
RAMBLER'S RETREAT	22				
OUSAL DALE	23				
OAKAMOOR	24				

AMENITIES GUIDE

VILLAGE	B&B	YHA	CAMP	INN	CAFE	SHOP	P.O.
OAKAMOOR	*		*	*	*	*	*
KINGSLEY HOLT				*		*	*
FROGHALL	*				*		
CAULDON LOW				*	*	*	*
STANTON	*		*				
ELLASTONE	*			*		*	
ALTON	*		*	*	*	*	*
OUSAL DALE		*			*		

INNS -

OAKAMOOR — Lord Nelson
　　　　　　　Cricketers Arms
　　　　　　　Admiral Jarvis Inn

KINGSLEY HOLT — Two inns just off route.

WHISTON — The Sneyds Arms, just off route.

CAULDON LOW — The Cross Inn.
　　　　　　　　The Green Man — just off route.

ELLASTONE — Duncombe Arms

ALTON — Royal Oak Inn
　　　　　Wild Duck Inn
　　　　　The Talbot Inn
　　　　　The Bull's Head
　　　　　The White Hart
　　　　　The Blacksmiths Arms

Y.H.A.

Dimmingsdale — Little Ranger, Oakamoor, Stoke on Trent, Staffs.
　　　　　　　ST10 3AS. Tel. 0538-702304.

CAMPSITES — basically open Easter to end of September.

COTTON, Nr Oakamoor — Star Farm, Cotton. Tel Oakamoor (0538) -
702219 . Grid Ref. SK067457

ALTON — Mrs G.V. Tideswell, Rainroach Farm. Tel Oakamoor (0538) -
702005. Grid Ref. SK063427

BED AND BREAKFAST — a random selection.

OAKAMOOR — Mrs M. Wheeler, Old Furnace Farm, Greendale.
Tel. Oakamoor (0538) — 702442

FROGHALL — The Hermitage. Tel Ipstones (053871) 515

STANTON — Mrs G.Tomlinson, Homes Close, Stanton, Ashbourne,
Derbys. Tel 033524 — 475

ALTON — Mrs E. Parker, 16 Shirley Drive, Alton.
Tel. 0538-590 947

　　　　　- Alverton, Denstone Lane, Alton.
　　　　　Tel. 0538 — 702265

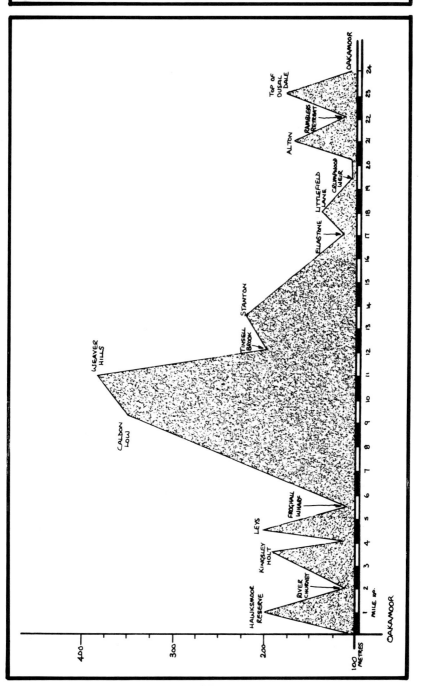

J M'S STAFFORDSHIRE CHALLENGE

Badges are Breton red cloth with figure embroidered in four colours and measure — 3" wide x 3½" high.

BADGE ORDER FORM

Date completed ....

Time ....

NAME ....

ADDRESS ....

....

Price: £1.75 each including postage, VAT and signed completion certificate.

From: J.N.M. Publications, Winster, Matlock, Derbyshire, DE4 2DQ
Tel: Winster (062988) 454 — 24hr answering service.

********* **You may photocopy this form if needed** ********

THE JOHN MERRILL WALK BADGE — walk this route twice or complete another John Merrill's challenge walk and send details and cheque/PO for £1.75 for a special circular walk badge. Price includes postage and VAT.

EQUIPMENT NOTES — some personal thoughts

BOOTS — preferably with a full leather upper, of medium weight, with a vibram sole. I always add a foam cushioned insole to help cushion the base of my feet.

SOCKS — I generally wear two thick pairs as this helps minimise blisters. The inner pair are of loop stitch variety and approximately 80% wool. The outer are a thick rib pair of approximately 80% wool.

WATERPROOFS — for general walking I wear a T shirt or shirt with a cotton wind jacket on top. You generate heat as you walk and I prefer to layer my clothes to avoid getting too hot. Depending on the season will dictate how many layers you wear. In soft rain I just use my wind jacket for I know it quickly dries out. In heavy downpours I slip on a neoprene lined cagoule, and although hot and clammy it does keep me reasonably dry. Only in extreme conditions will I don overtrousers, much preferring to get wet and feel comfortable.

FOOD — as I walk I carry bars of chocolate, for they provide instant energy and are light to carry. In winter a flask of hot coffee is welcome. I never carry water and find no hardship from doing so, but this is a personal matter! From experience I find the more I drink the more I want and sweat. You should always carry some extra food such as Kendal mint cake, for emergencies.

RUCKSACKS — for day walking I use a climbing rucksac of about 40 litre capacity and although it leaves excess space it does mean that the sac is well padded, with an internal frame and padded shoulder straps. Inside apart from the basics for the day I carry gloves, balaclava, spare pullover and a pair of socks.

MAP & COMPASS — when I am walking I always have the relevant map — preferably the 1:25,000 scale — open in my hand. This enables me to constantly check that I am walking the right way. In case of bad weather I carry a compass, which once mastered gives you complete confidence in thick cloud or mist.

ROCKS NEAR UPPER COTTON

REMEMBER AND OBSERVE THE COUNTRY CODE

Enjoy the countryside and respect its life and work.

Guard against all risk of fire.

Fasten all gates.

Keep your dogs under close conrrol.

Keep to public paths across farmland.

Use gates and stiles to cross fences, hedges and walls.

Leave livestock, crops and machinery alone.

Take your litter home — pack it in, pack it out.

Help to keep all water clean.

Protect wildlife, plants and trees.

Take special care on country roads.

Make no unnecessary noise.

CRUMPWOOD WEIR

ABOUT THE WALK -

Whilst every care is taken detailing and describing the walk in this book, it should be borne in mind that the countryside changes by the seasons and the work of man. I have described the walks to the best of my ability, detailing what I have found on the walk in the way of stiles and signs. Obviously with the passage of time stiles become broken or replaced by a ladder stile or even a small gate. Signs too have a habit of being broken or pushed over. All the route follows rights of way and only on rare occasions will you have to overcome obstacles in its path, such as a barbed wire fence or electric fence.

The seasons bring occasional problems whilst out walking which should also be bourne in mind. In the height of summer paths become overgrown and you will have to fight your way through in a few places. In low lying areas the fields are full of crops, and although the pathline goes straight across it may be more practical to walk round the field edge to get to the next stile or gate. In summer the ground is generally dry but in autumn and winter, especially because of our climate, the surface can be decidedly wet and slippery; sometimes even glutonous mud!

These comments are part of countryside walking which help to make your walk more interesting or briefly frustrating. Standing in a farmyard up to your ankles in mud might not be funny at the time but upon reflection was one of the highlights of the walk!

THE HIKER'S CODE

* **Hike only along marked routes — do not leave the trail.**

* **Use stiles to climb fences; close gates.**

* **Camp only in designated campsites.**

* **Carry a light-weight stove.**

* **Leave the Trail cleaner than you found it.**

* **Leave flowers and plants for others to enjoy.**

* **Keep dogs on a leash.**

* **Protect and do not disturb wildlife.**

* **Use the trail at your own risk.**

* **Leave only your thanks — take nothing but photographs.**

OTHER CHALLENGE WALKS BY JOHN N. MERRILL -

DAY CHALLENGES -

John Merrill's Peak District Challenge Walk — 25 miles.
Circular walk from Bakewell involving 3,600 feet of ascent.

John Merrill's Yorkshire Dales Challenge Walk — 23 miles.
Circular walk from Kettlewell involving 3,600 feet of ascent.

John Merrill's North Yorkshire Moors Challenge Walk — 24 miles.
Circular walk from Goathland — a seaside bash — involving 2,000 feet of ascent.

The Little John Challenge Walk — 28 miles.
Circular walk from Edwinstowe in Sherwood Forest — Robin Hood country.

Peak District End to End Walks.
1. Gritstone Edge Walk — 23 miles down the eastern edge system.
2. Limestone Dale Walk — 24 miles down the limestone dales from Buxton to Ashbourne.

Forthcoming titles —

John Merrill's Peak District Challenge Walk No 2 — The Dark Peak Challenge.

John Merrill's Snowdonia Challenge Walk.

MULTIPLE DAY CHALLENGE WALKS -

The Limey Way — 40 miles
Down twenty limestone dales from Castleton to Thorpe in the Peak District.

The Peakland Way — 100 miles.
John Merrill's classic walk around the Peak District.

The River's Way — 43 miles.
Down the five main river systems of the Peak District, from Edale, the end of the Pennine Way, to Ilam.

Peak District High Level Route — 90 miles
Circular walk from Matlock taking in the highest and remotest parts of the Peak District.

OTHER BOOKS BY JOHN N. MERRILL PUBLISHED BY JNM PUBLICATIONS

DAY WALK GUIDES -

SHORT CIRCULAR WALKS IN THE PEAK DISTRICT
LONG CIRCULAR WALKS IN THE PEAK DISTRICT
CIRCULAR WALKS IN WESTERN PEAKLAND
SHORT CIRCULAR WALKS IN THE STAFFORDSHIRE MOORLANDS
PEAK DISTRICT TOWN WALKS
SHORT CIRCULAR WALKS AROUND MATLOCK
SHORT CIRCULAR WALKS IN THE DUKERIES
SHORT CIRCULAR WALKS IN SOUTH YORKSHIRE
SHORT CIRCULAR WALKS AROUND DERBY
SHORT CIRCULAR WALKS AROUND BUXTON
SHORT CIRCULAR WALKS AROUND NOTTINGHAMSHIRE
SHORT CIRCULAR WALKS ON THE NORTHERN MOORS
40 SHORT CIRCULAR PEAK DISTRICT WALKS
SHORT CIRCULAR WALKS IN THE HOPE VALLEY

INSTRUCTION & RECORD -

HIKE TO BE FIT..STROLLING WITH JOHN
THE JOHN MERRILL WALK RECORD BOOK

CANAL WALK GUIDES -

VOL ONE — DERBYSHIRE AND NOTTINGHAMSHIRE
VOL TWO — CHESHIRE AND STAFFORDSHIRE
VOL THREE — STAFFORDSHIRE
VOL FOUR — THE CHESHIRE RING

DAY CHALLENGE WALKS -

JOHN MERRILL'S PEAK DISTRICT CHALLENGE WALK
JOHN MERRILL'S YORKSHIRE DALES CHALLENGE WALK
JOHN MERRILL'S NORTH YORKSHIRE MOORS CHALLENGE WALK
PEAK DISTRICT END TO END WALKS
THE LITTLE JOHN CHALLENGE WALK
JOHN MERRILL'S LAKELAND CHALLENGE WALK
JOHN MERRILL'S STAFFORDSHIRE MOORLAND CHALLENGE WALK
JOHN MERRILL'S DARK PEAK CHALLENGE WALK

MULTIPLE DAY WALKS -

THE RIVERS' WAY
PEAK DISTRICT HIGH LEVEL ROUTE
PEAK DISTRICT MARATHONS
THE LIMEY WAY
THE PEAKLAND WAY

COAST WALKS -

ISLE OF WIGHT COAST WALK
PEMBROKESHIRE COAST PATH
THE CLEVELAND WAY

HISTORICAL GUIDES -

DERBYSHIRE INNS
HALLS AND CASTLES OF THE PEAK DISTRICT & DERBYSHIRE
TOURING THE PEAK DISTRICT AND DERBYSHIRE BY CAR
DERBYSHIRE FOLKLORE
LOST INDUSTRIES OF DERBYSHIRE
PUNISHMENT IN DERBYSHIRE
CUSTOMS OF THE PEAK DISTRICT AND DERBYSHIRE
WINSTER — A VISITOR'S GUIDE
ARKWRIGHT OF CROMFORD
TALES FROM THE MINES by GEOFFREY CARR
PEAK DISTRICT PACE NAMES by MARTIN SPRAY

JOHN'S MARATHON WALKS -

TURN RIGHT AT LAND'S END
WITH MUSTARD ON MY BACK
TURN RIGHT AT DEATH VALLEY
EMERALD COAST WALK

COLOUR GUIDES -

THE PEAK DISTRICT ....Something to remember her by.

SKETCH BOOKS — by John Creber

NORTH STAFFORDSHIRE SKETCHBOOK